D0996487

Facts About Countries

Bangladesh

Michael March

First published in 2005 by
Franklin Watts
96 Leonard Street, London
EC2A 4XD

Franklin Watts Australia
Level 17/207 Kent Street
Sydney NSW 2000

Facts About Countries is based on the Country Files series published by Franklin Watts. It is produced for Franklin Watts by Bender Richardson White, PO Box 266, Uxbridge, UK.
Editor: Lionel Bender
Designer and Page Make-up: Ben White
Picture Researcher: Cathy Stastny
Cover Make-up: Mike Pilley, Radius
Production: Kim Richardson

Graphics and Maps: Stefan Chabluk
Educational Advisor: Prue Goodwin, Institute of Education, The University of Reading
Consultant: Dr Terry Jennings, a former geography teacher and university lecturer. He is now a full-time writer of children's geography and science books.

A CIP catalogue record for this book is available from the British Library.

ISBN 0-7496-6032-5
Dewey Classification 915.492

Printed in China

Picture Credits

Pages 1: Corbis Images/Roger Wood. 3: James Davis Travel Photography. 4: Robert Harding/Liba Taylor. 7: Hutchison/Liba Taylor. 8: Hutchison/Dirk. R. Frans. 9, 11: Hutchison/Liba Taylor. 12-13: James Davis Travel Photography. 14: Hutchison/Dirk R. Frans. 15: James Davis Travel Photography. 17 top: Hutchison/Dirk R. Frans. 17 bottom: Hutchison/Liba Taylor. 18: Robert Harding Photo Library. 19: Hutchison/Liba Taylor. 20: Panos Pictures/Zed Nelson. 21: Hutchison Library. 22-23: Robert Harding/Liba Taylor. 23: Hutchison/ Trevor Page. 24: Hutchison/Bruce Wills. 25: Corbis Images/Roger Wood. 26-27: James Davis Travel Photography. 28: Robert Harding/Nigel Cromm. 30: Hutchison/Dirk R. Frans. 31: Hutchison Library. Cover Photo: Eye Ubiquitous.

The Author

Michael March is a full-time writer and editor of non-fiction books. He has written more than 20 books for children about different countries of the world.

Note to parents and teachers

Every effort has been made by the Publishers to ensure that the websites in this book are suitable for children, that they are of the highest educational value, and that they contain no inappropriate or offensive material. However, because of the nature of the Internet, it is impossible to guarantee that the contents of these sites will not be altered. We strongly advise that Internet access is supervised by a responsible adult.

Contents

Welcome to Bangladesh

Bangladesh is a country in southern Asia. It is about the size of England and Wales put together. The land is mostly flat and often gets flooded.

Land of the Bengali people

The Bengalis are an ancient people, with a history going back thousands of years. Some 30 years ago, they set up their own independent country, Bangladesh. Before 1971, the region was part of Pakistan. Bangladeshis are famous for handicrafts such as cotton clothes, embroidered silk robes and delicate jewellery.

DATABASE

Neighbours

Bangladesh is surrounded by its huge neighbour, India. To the south is a 580-kilometre-long coastline on the Bay of Bengal. To the south-east lies the country Myanmar, or Burma.

Below. **The capital city, Dhaka (which used to be spelled Dacca) is crowded, busy and noisy.**

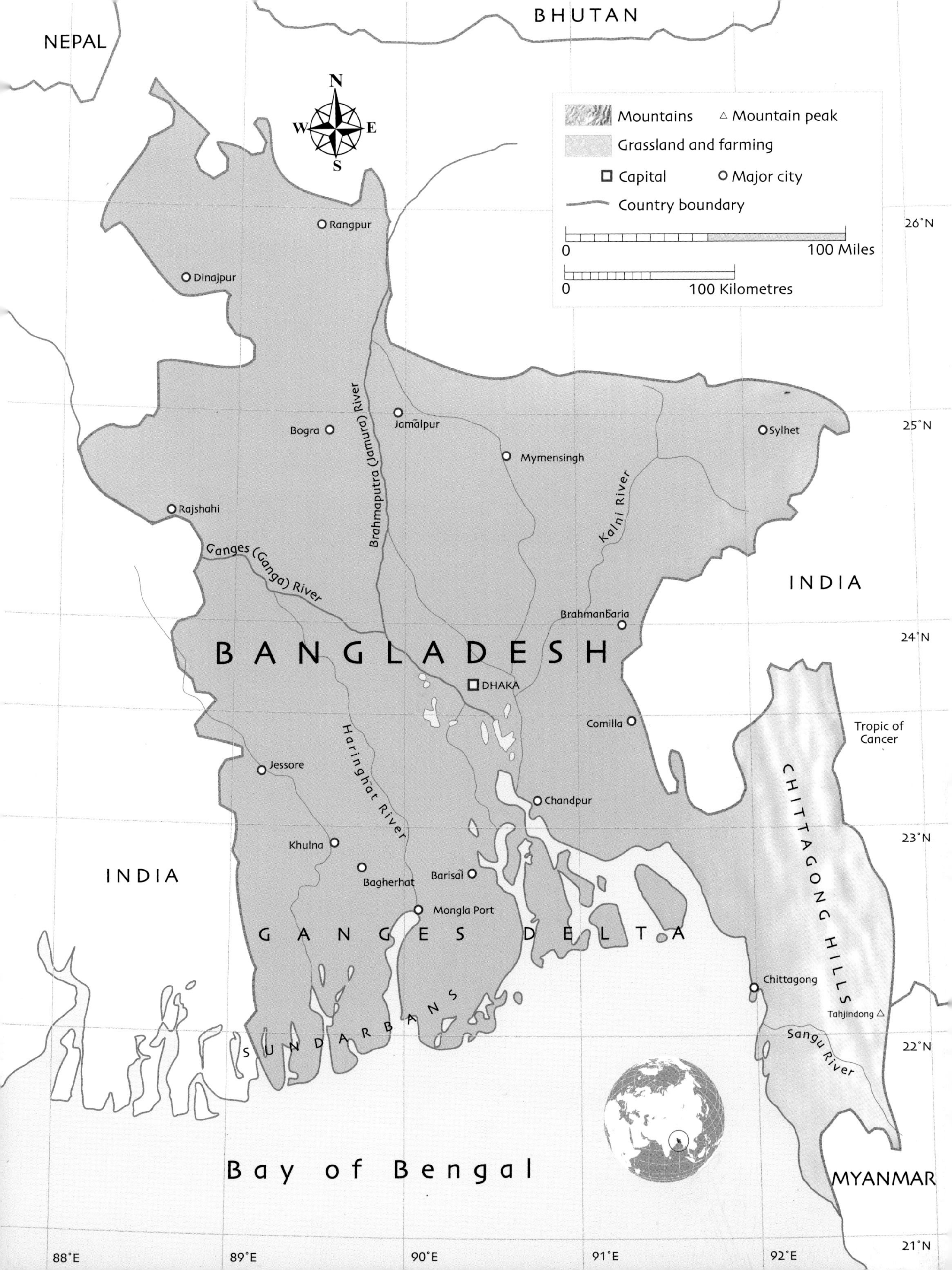
NEPAL
BHUTAN
N
W
E
S
Mountains
Mountain peak
Grassland and farming
Capital
Major city
Country boundary
0
100 Miles
0
100 Kilometres
26°N
Rangpur
Dinajpur
Brahmaputra (Jamura) River
Jamalpur
Bogra
25°N
Sylhet
Mymensingh
Kalni River
Rajshahi
Ganges (Ganga) River
INDIA
Brahmanbaria
24°N
BANGLADESH
DHAKA
Comilla
Tropic of Cancer
Haringhat River
Jessore
Chandpur
CHITTAGONG HILLS
23°N
Khulna
INDIA
Bagherhat
Barisal
Mongla Port
GANGES DELTA
Chittagong
SUNDARBANS
Tahjindong
22°N
Sangu River
Bay of Bengal
MYANMAR
21°N
88°E
89°E
90°E
91°E
92°E

The Land

Plants and Animals

Elephants and leopards live in the forests of the Chittagong Hills. The Sundarbans, in the south-west, is the world's largest mangrove forest. It is the home of the Bengal tiger. Altogether, Bangladesh has some 200 species of mammals, 120 species of reptiles, 700 species of birds and 200 species of fish.

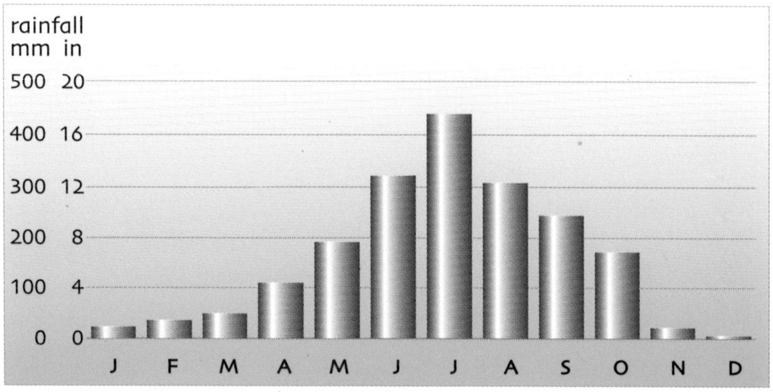

Much of Bangladesh is low-lying land around the rivers Brahmaputra and Ganges. Flooding from the rivers and the sea has created a very fertile soil.

Hill country

Only about a tenth of Bangladesh is hilly. Most of the hills are in the south-east. Forests grow on some of the higher areas.

rainfall
mm in
500 20
400 16
300 12
200 8
100 4
0 0
J F M A M J J A S O N D

Above. **How much rain falls each month in Dhaka.**

Rainfall

Rainfall is highest in the north-east. As much as 635 cm of rain may fall there in a year.

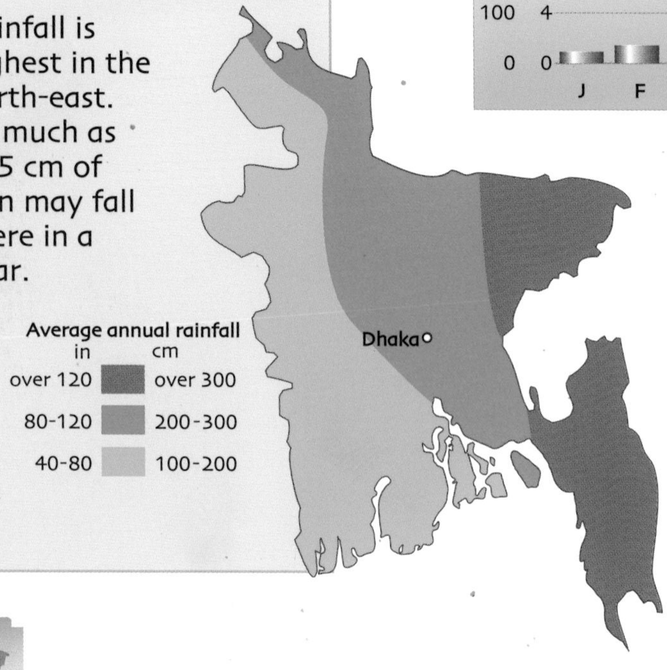

Average annual rainfall
in cm
over 120 over 300
80-120 200-300
40-80 100-200

Dhaka

Climate

In Bangladesh it is warm, or hot and damp all year round. The east of the country gets about three times as much rain as the west. Most of the rain falls between May and September, during the monsoon, when a third of the country becomes flooded. At other times, there are droughts.

Between April and October there are sometimes violent storms along the coast. In 1970, a storm killed about 500,000 people. In 1991 another storm cost 120,000 lives and left millions of people homeless.

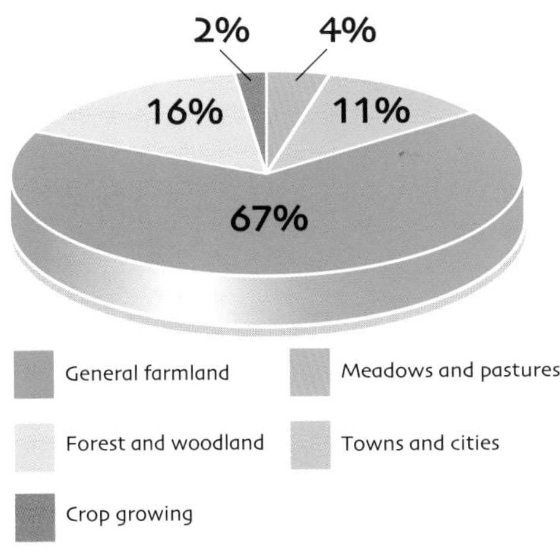

Above. **How land is used in Bangladesh.**

Below. **In the countryside, most houses have a thatched or corrugated iron roof.**

Web Search ▶▶

- **www.bangladeshonline.com/bmd/** Bangladesh's climate and weather.
- **www.worldinfozone.com/country.php?country=Bangladesh** Information on Bangladesh's climate, plants and animals.
- **www.discoverybangladesh.com/dream_dest_chittagong.html** Tourist information about Chittagong.

The People

Bangladesh has about 133 million people. It is the world's seventh-largest country in terms of population.

A mix of peoples

Most Bengalis originally came from the regions that are today Myanmar, northern India, and Tibet in China. They mixed and bred with the local people of different races and religions.

Below. **In the towns, the streets are crowded with rickshaws.**

Language

The official language of Bangladesh is Bangla. It is also called Bengali and is spoken by all Bengalis. It is based on an ancient language called Sanskrit.

English is also widely used in Bangladesh. Many of the people who came to Bangladesh from India in the late 1940s also speak and write in the Urdu language.

Above. Native Bengalis often have dark skin and black hair. They are usually of medium height and build.

Right. Numbers of men and women in Bangladesh.

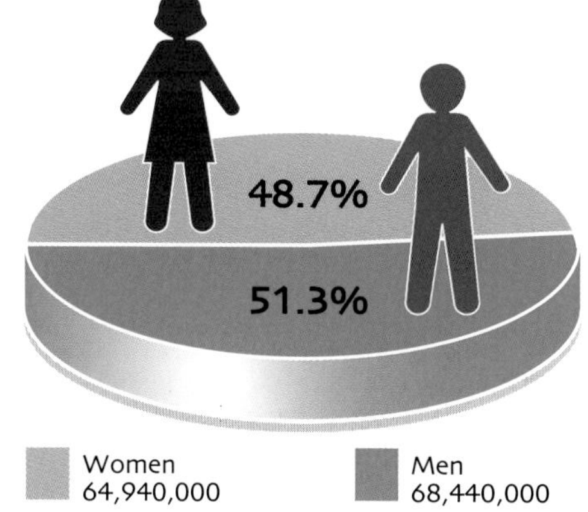

Age groups

Bangladesh is a young country. More than a third of the population is under 15 years of age, and half under 25. Only about 3 per cent of people are aged 65 or older.

Boys outnumber girls, and men outnumber women, in every age group. The biggest difference between numbers of men and women is in the over 65s, where there are about 10 per cent more men than women. Overall, Bangladeshi men outnumber women by five per cent. Fifty years ago, this difference was nearly 10 per cent.

Web Search ▶▶

- **www.discoverybangladesh.com/meetbangladesh/statistic.html**
  Facts and figures about the population of Bangladesh.
- **www.bbsgov.org/**
  Bangladesh government's Bureau of Statistics.

Town and Country Life

On average, 920 people live on every square kilometre of Bangladesh. It is one of the most densely populated countries on Earth. The population is growing by between 1.5 and 2 per cent a year.

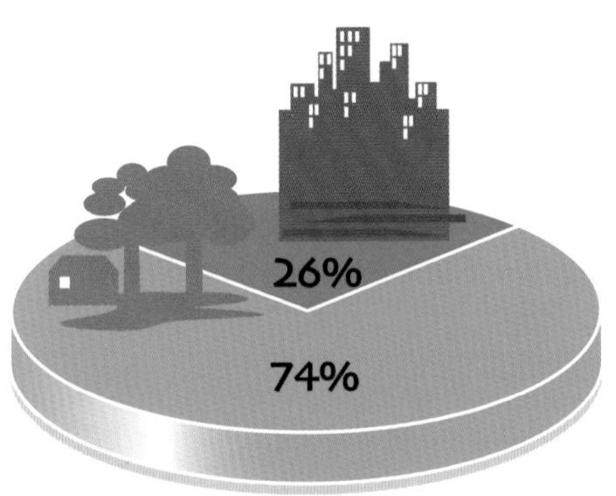

Percentage of population living in cities and towns

Percentage of population living in the countryside

Above. Where people live.

Where people live

About 9 million people live in Dhaka. It is by far the biggest city. The Chittagong Hills and the Sundarbans, a region of swamps, have fewer people than other areas – only about 30 people per square kilometre. About three-quarters of the population live in the countryside but many people are now moving to the towns.

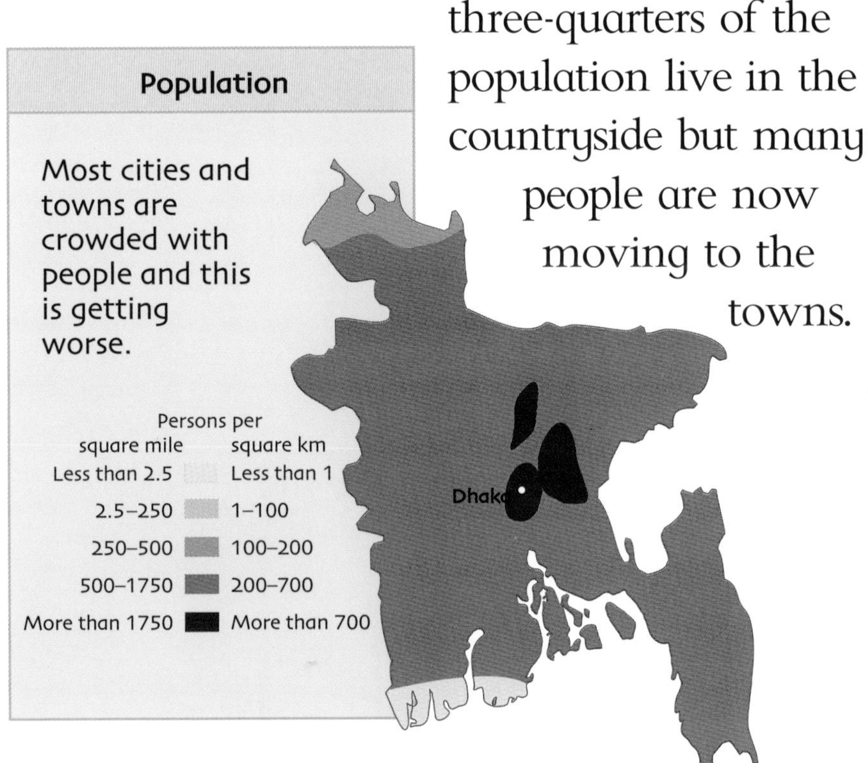

Clothing

Many Bangladeshi men wear the traditional *lungi*, a kind of skirt, and often go barefoot. Most women wear the traditional *saree*, a wide strip of cotton or silk that is wrapped round the body and draped over a shoulder.

Houses and homes

In the countryside, villagers build small houses of bamboo, with one or two rooms for a family. Most houses have no electricity. In times of serious flooding, people move on to the roof or live in small boats.

In the towns and cities, some families have brick or concrete homes or live in small apartment buildings. But many live crowded together in small wooden houses.

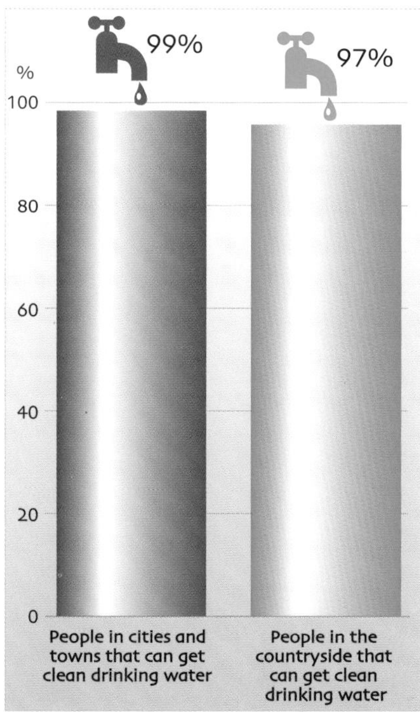

Below. **In the countryside, most people get their drinking water from wells.**

Right. **Almost everyone can get clean drinking water, but few homes have plumbing.**

- **www.discoverybangladesh.com/meetbangladesh/demographic_feature.html**
  Website about where people live in Bangladesh.
- **www.world-gazetteer.com/**
  Information on populations of cities, towns and regions of Bangladesh.
- **www.bangladeshonline.com/tourism/popu.htm**
  Facts and figures on visitors to and from Bangladesh.

Farming and Fishing

More than half the workers of Bangladesh work on the land. Most of them are rice farmers. Rice and fish are the main foods that people eat.

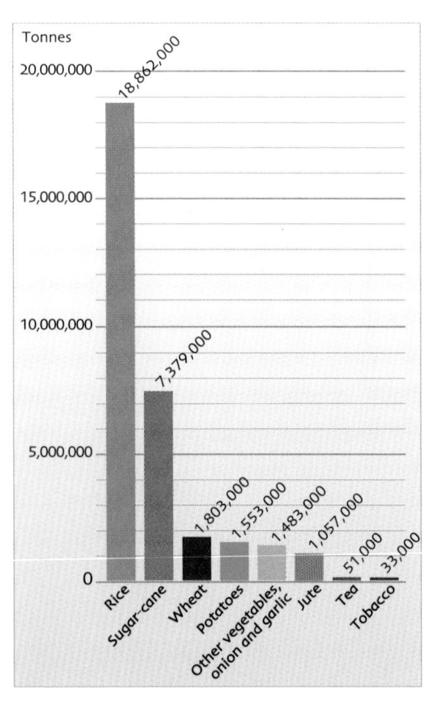

Above. **The different crops grown in Bangladesh.**

Main crops

Many of the 17 million farmers own small areas of land – about the size of three football pitches. They farm using hand tools and animals such as bullocks. In areas where it is hot and wet, rice can be grown and harvested three times each year. The main crops grown for export are tea and jute. Jute is used to make rope and mats.

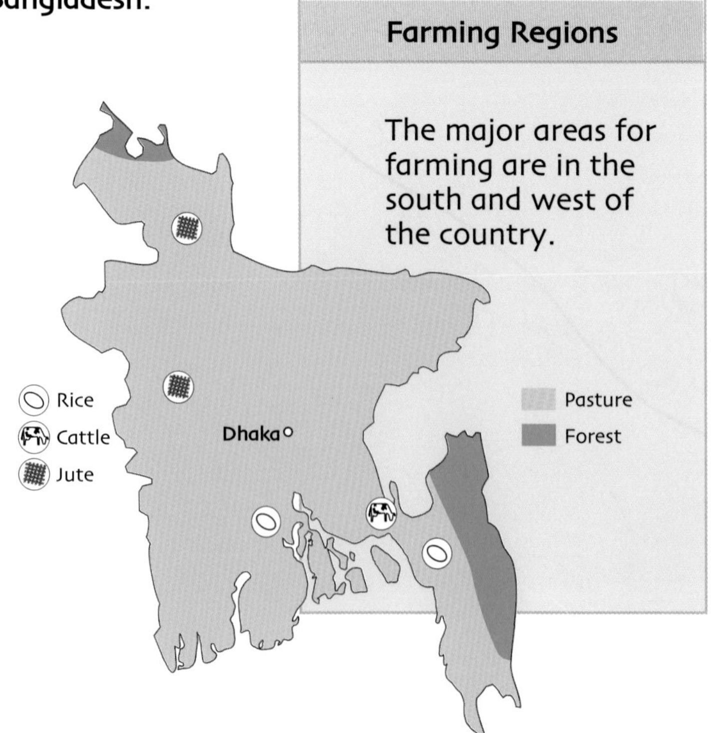

Fruit, leather, fish and shellfish

Farmers also grow vegetables, sugar-cane and a wide variety of fruit, including mangoes and bananas. Cattle are kept mainly for the leather from their skins.

Over a million Bangladeshis fish for a living. Hilsa, a kind of herring, and prawns are the main fish catch. Prawns are also farmed in special ponds for export. Catfish, carp and other species are fished in the country's many rivers.

Shift and Burn

Some Bangladeshis make land for farming by cutting down trees and burning them. They use the ashes as fertilizer. They then sow the seeds and harvest the crop, before moving on to another patch. The first patch is then left to return to grass or forest.

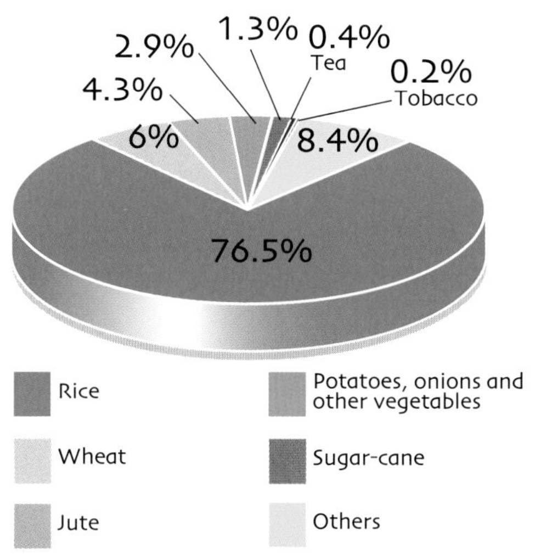

Above. **Crops grown, by weight.**

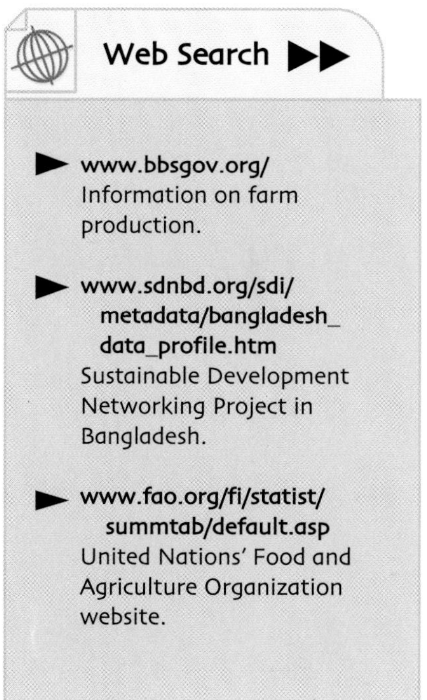

Web Search

- **www.bbsgov.org/** Information on farm production.
- **www.sdnbd.org/sdi/metadata/bangladesh_data_profile.htm** Sustainable Development Networking Project in Bangladesh.
- **www.fao.org/fi/statist/summtab/default.asp** United Nations' Food and Agriculture Organization website.

Left. **Fishermen unload their catch of freshwater fish on a riverbank in Dhaka.**

Resources and Industry

DATABASE

Cheap labour

Many factories produce clothing and knitwear, which are major exports. Other factories turn jute into burlap (for making sacks), or make leather goods and steel. Service industries include banking, hotels, transport and catering. Labour is cheap. Many workers are paid less than £1 a day.

About one third of Bangladeshi workers work in factories, or in industries such as banking, transport and tourism, which are called service industries.

Energy supplies

Bangladesh has more than twenty gas fields, some of them offshore in the Bay of Bengal. Natural gas and coal provide 90 per cent of the country's electricity. The rest comes from hydro-electric power from the country's rivers.

Below. **Sewing in a clothes factory.**

Right. **Output of manufactured goods.**

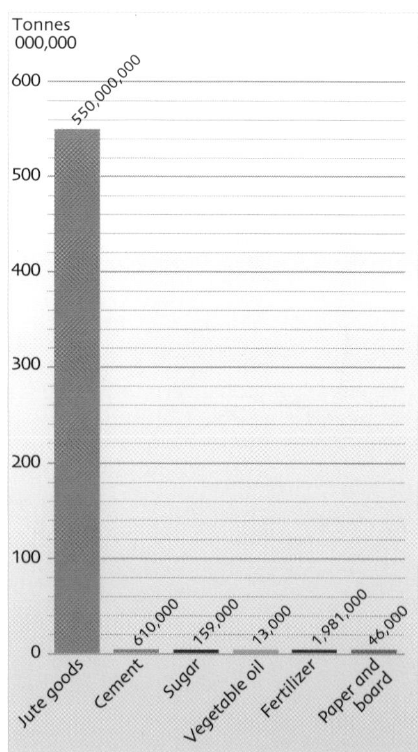

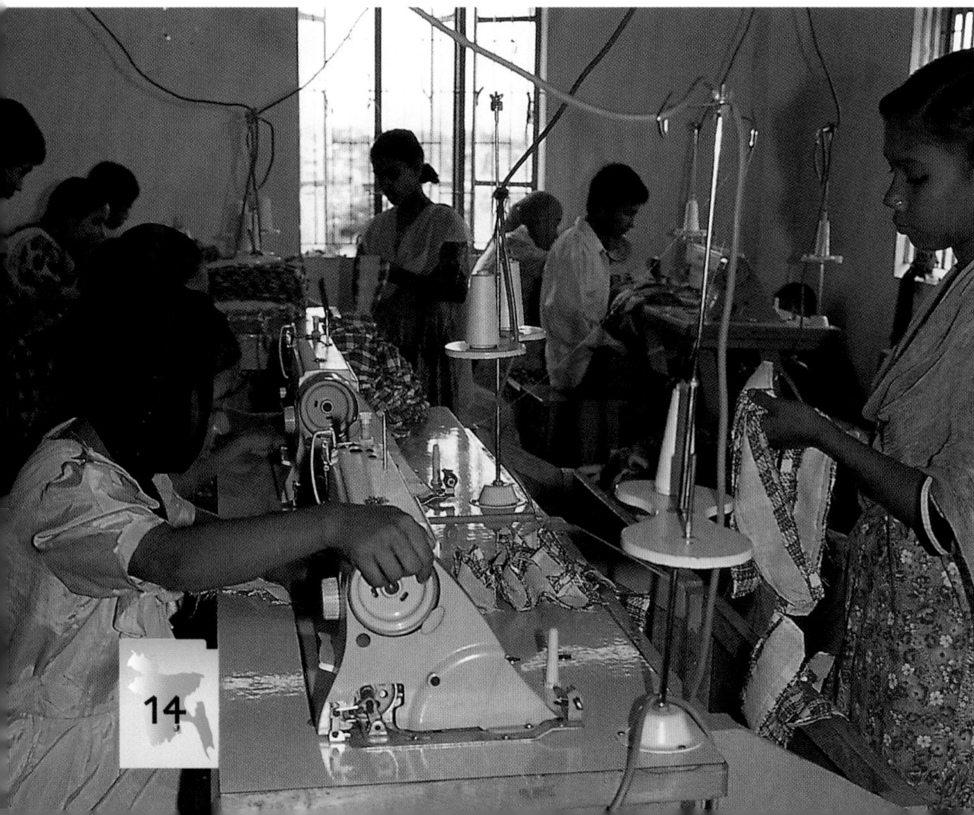

Using resources

Most of the fuel used in homes for heating and cooking comes from wood, animal dung or crop waste. The rest comes from oil.

Natural gas is used to make fertilizer, a major export. Sand is used in glass-making. Limestone and hard rock provide cement and other materials used to make buildings. Bamboo is pulped to make paper.

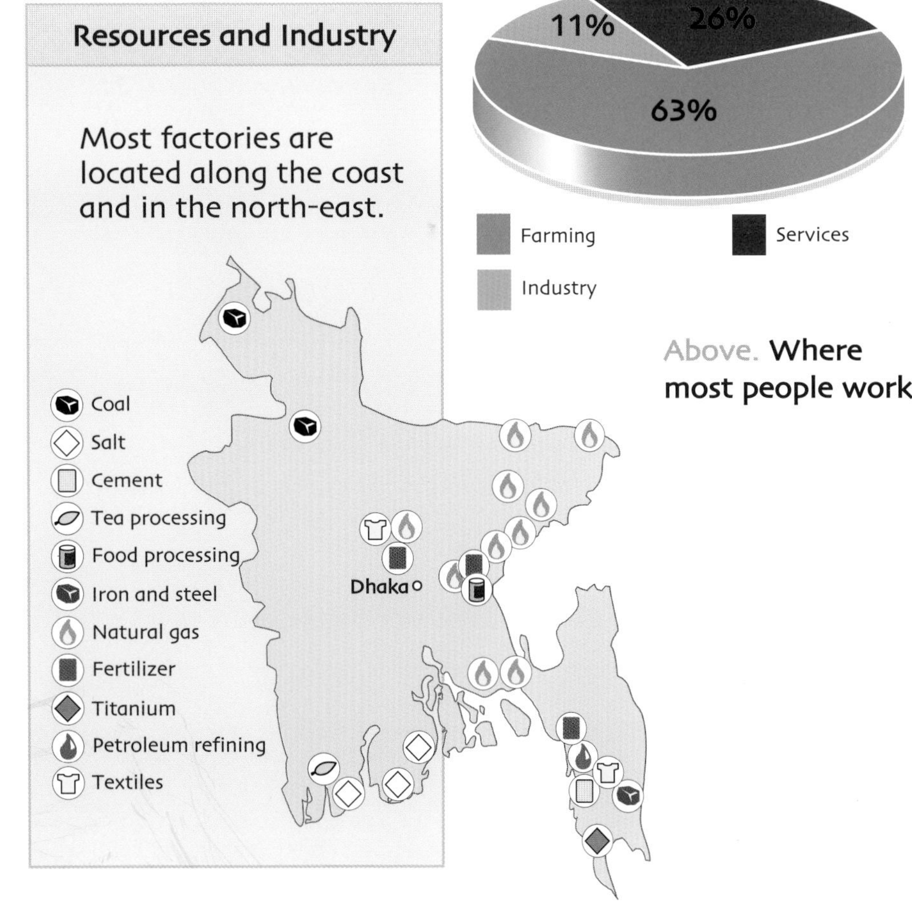

Above. **Where most people work.**

Below. **At a brickworks outside Dhaka, firewood is burned to heat ovens in which the bricks are baked.**

Web Search ▶▶

- **www.virtualbangladesh.com/economy/**
  Information about Bangladeshi industry.
- **www.bbsgov.org/**
  Government facts and figures on industry.
- **www.discoverybangladesh.com/meetbangladesh/economy.html**
  Website about energy and industry.

Transport

Biman, Bangladesh's airline, flies to different cities in the country and abroad. Most journeys in Bangladesh are made by road, railway or waterway.

Different forms of transport

Bangladesh has cargo ships, container ships and oil tankers. Most of the country's imports and exports go through the seaports of Chittagong and Mongla. Over 1,400 ships call at Chittagong harbour every year, and Mongla handles over 300 ships a year.

Inland, river ports are also important. During the monsoon season, there are 8,000 kilometres of waterways that can be used by boats. During the dry season, however, this shrinks to 5,000 kilometres.

Today, most passengers and goods in Bangladesh go by road. Bus services link all the main towns.

The railways, which are owned by the state, run 300 locomotives, 1,200 passenger coaches and 16,000 freight wagons between more than 500 stations.

Bicycles and Rickshaws

40 per cent of all journeys in Dhaka are made by bicycle. Dhaka has 600,000 bicycle rickshaws – colourfully decorated passenger vehicles that are based on a bicycle. These are used both by local people and by tourists. Autorickshaws are similar but motorized, and are therefore quicker.

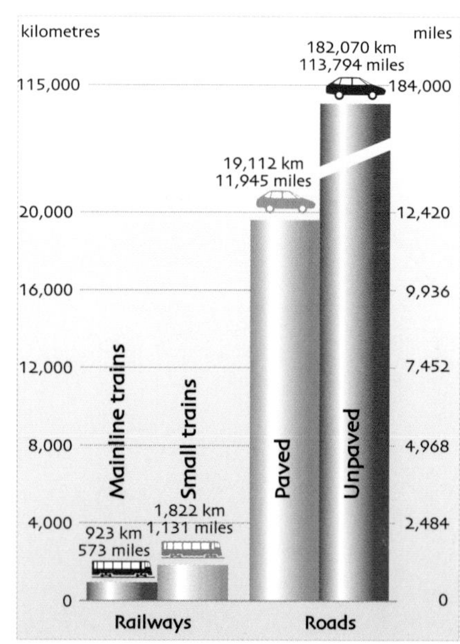

Above. **The lengths of the rail and road systems.**

ove. Mainline trains, like this one Dhaka, are larger than the trains ed in the countryside.

Below. In the countryside, wooden rafts are used as ferryboats.

Transport

All the transport systems are centred on Dhaka, the capital city.

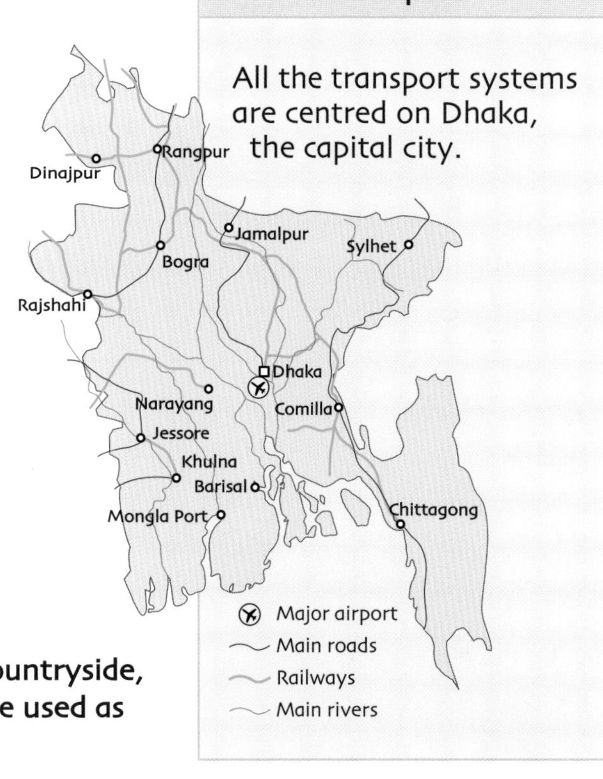

Web Search ▶▶

- www.bbsgov.org/ Government information about transport.
- www.bimanair.com/ Biman, the national airline of Bangladesh.
- www.discoverybangladesh.com/transportation.html Information about Bangladesh's transport systems.

Education

In Bangladesh, children go to primary school from age 6 to 11. Many go on to secondary school until 16. A few stay at school until 18 and then enter university.

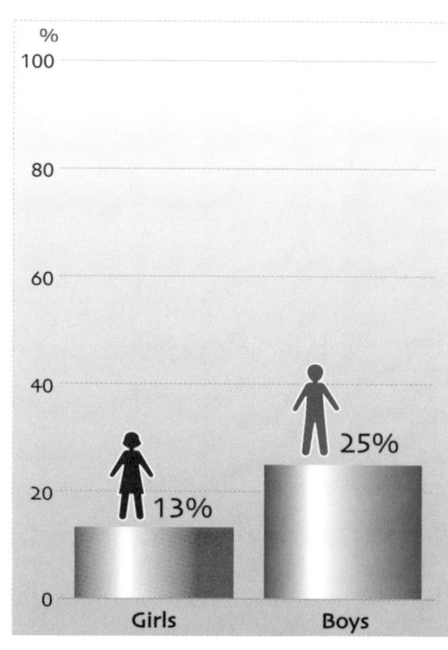

Above. Percentages of boys and girls who go on to secondary education.

Primary and secondary schools

All children must go to primary school, which is free. Children study Bangla, English, maths and science. They are also taught skills to help their parents at home.

Secondary education is not generally free and many children do not attend. But the government pays for some girls to stay at school so they do not give up their studies to marry young. Schools called *madrasas* are religious. There, the religion of Islam is taught as well as other subjects.

Right. A classroom in a village school.

University education

Secondary schools in cities are the best equipped. Often, village schools have too few teachers and not many books.

Children who want to go to university or to a college of technology must pass the School and Higher School Certificate exams. The University of Dhaka is the largest in Bangladesh.

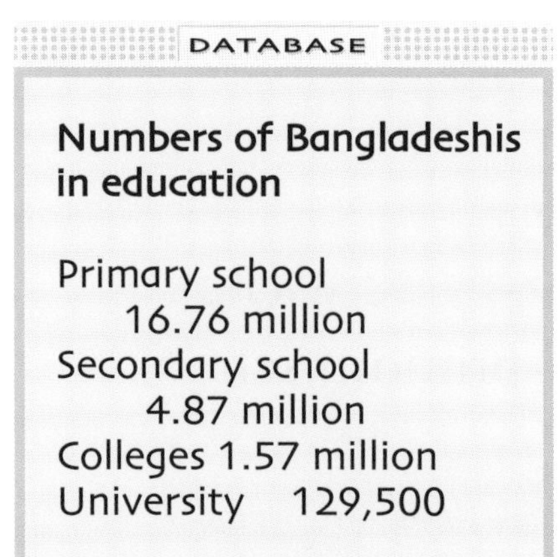
DATABASE

Numbers of Bangladeshis in education

Primary school
16.76 million
Secondary school
4.87 million
Colleges 1.57 million
University 129,500

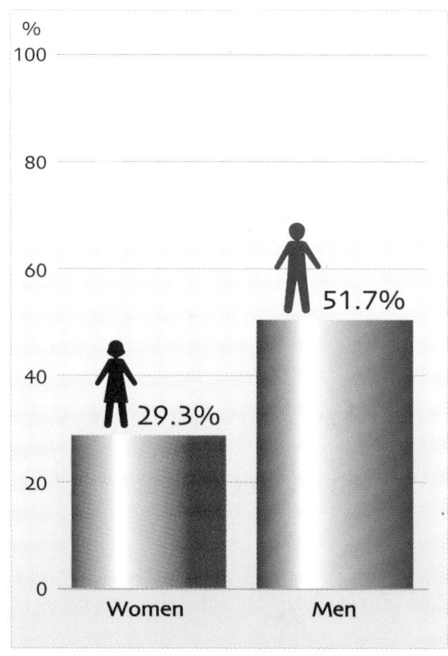

Above. **Bangladeshis who can read and write.**

Below. **Young women being taught how to embroider clothes.**

Web Search ▶▶

- **www.unicef.org/infobycountry/bangladesh_statistics.html**
  UNESCO International Bureau of Education survey.
- **www.unicef.org/girlseducation/index.html**
  UNESCO facts about girls' education worldwide.

Sport and Leisure

Among Bangladeshis, cricket, hockey and football are the most popular sports. Kabbadi is the national game.

Traditional sports

Kabbadi (see below) began as a way of developing self-defence skills among unarmed people. Another traditional sport is boat racing. Every year, on rivers and canals, teams of villagers race against each other in colourful rowing boats.

Below. **Children practise their footballing skills watched by their teacher.**

DATABASE

Bangabandhu Stadium

International cricket has been played at the Dhaka stadium since 1955. In 1971, the stadium was renamed the Bangabandhu Stadium in honour of Bangabandhu Sheikh Mujibur-Rahman, who founded Bangladesh as an independent country.

Kabbadi

This traditional game is like 'touch-rugby' but without a ball. It lasts 40 minutes. 'Raiders' go one at a time into their opponents' half of the court to touch the 'enemy'. The raider must return to his half without drawing another breath. If he succeeds, then the players he touches are 'out'. But if his enemy holds him so that he cannot get back before drawing breath, then it is the raider who is 'out'.

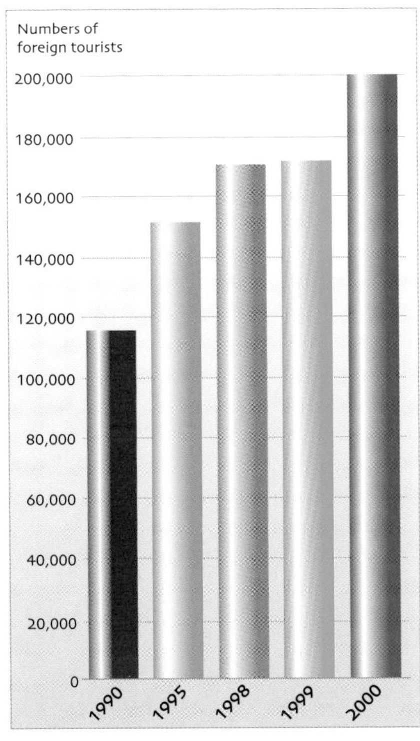

Above. **Tourists visiting Bangladesh**

Above. **At a school sports gala, students perform a traditional martial arts display.**

A sporting nation

In 2000, Bangladesh was recognized in cricket as a test match side. The country also made history in chess by producing, in 1986, the first Grandmaster from the Indian subcontinent.

Some 30 National Sports Federations run cricket, hockey, football, tennis, boxing, cycling and basketball across the country. Women have separate sports federations.

Web Search ▶▶

- **www.abyznewslinks.com/bangl.htm**
  Information about sport in Bangladeshi newspapers.
- **www.aboutaball.co.uk/html2/countries/bangladesh.php**
  Football in Bangladesh.
- **www.gamecricket.com/asia-cup-bangladesh-team.html**
  Cricket in Bangladesh.

Daily Life and Religion

The nation's health and welfare services are improving and people are living longer. But wages are low and electrical goods, such as televisions, are expensive.

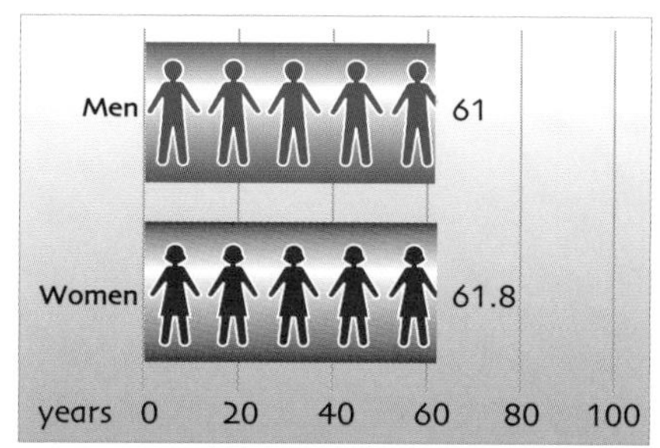

Above. The average age Bangladeshis can expect to live to.

Healthcare

Healthcare in Bangladesh is improving, with 70 per cent of children now being protected against diseases such as polio and diphtheria, compared with just 55 per cent 10 years ago.

Welfare services are now being developed to help pregnant women, disabled people, senior citizens and the unemployed.

Religion

Most Bangladeshis are Muslims. They follow the religion of Islam. Each day, Muslims visit their local mosque to pray. A mosque is a Muslim house of worship.

Right. A street trader in Dhaka. Most people buy their food, clothes and household goods from market stalls and small shops.

Poverty

More than one third of the population of Bangladesh is poor. Most people there earn about £240 a year, so they cannot afford to buy luxuries such as a television set or a computer. To buy a second-hand car would take more than 20 years' savings for a typical Bangladeshi.

Above. **A Buddhist temple in a village in Chittagong.**

Right. **Followers of the main religions.**

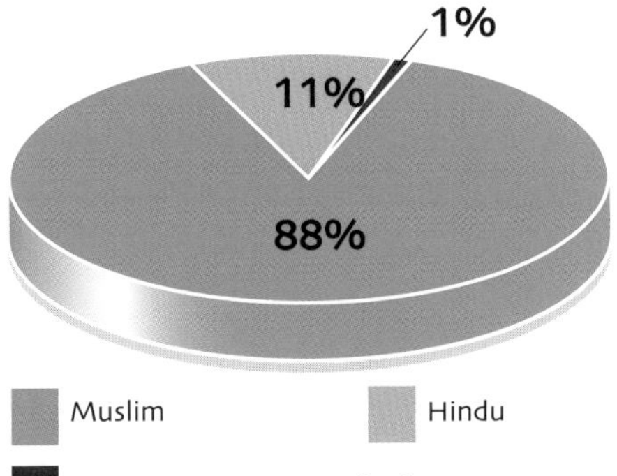

The Working Week

Shops and offices open between 9.00 a.m. and 5.00 p.m., Saturday to Friday. Sunday is a normal working day, and Friday is a day off for Muslim worship.

Web Search ▶▶

► **www.citechco.net/bangladesh/religion.html**
Information about religion in Bangladesh.

Arts and Media

Bangladesh is well-known for its art, architecture, dance, drama and music.

Old and new

The most beautiful buildings in the country are mosques and temples that are hundreds of years old. They are covered with carvings and decorations. Bengali artists usually paint scenes of everyday life. The most famous paintings are by Zainul Abedin. Bengali writer Rabindranath Tagore (1861-1941) won the Nobel Prize for Literature in 1913.

DATABASE

Cinema

The first full-length Bangladeshi feature film was made in 1956. Today, the country makes about 60 films a year. *The Clay Bird*, a film released in 2003, was very popular. The film tells the story of a boy growing up in Bangladesh in the 1960s when it was struggling for independence.

Below. **Posters for a Bangladeshi film at a cinema in Dhaka.**

Singing

Traditional folk songs in the styles called *jari* and *shari* are sung while instruments such as the *banshi* (bamboo flute) and *eklara* (a single-stringed lute) are played. Men and women perform a dance to the music.

Above. **A woman performs a traditional dance.**

The media

About 200 daily newspapers are published in Bangladesh. Some 37 per cent of people have access to a radio, but only about 10 per cent to a television. Radio and TV stations are run by the government, but there are also commercial and satellite stations.

Below. **Television and radio broadcast stations.**

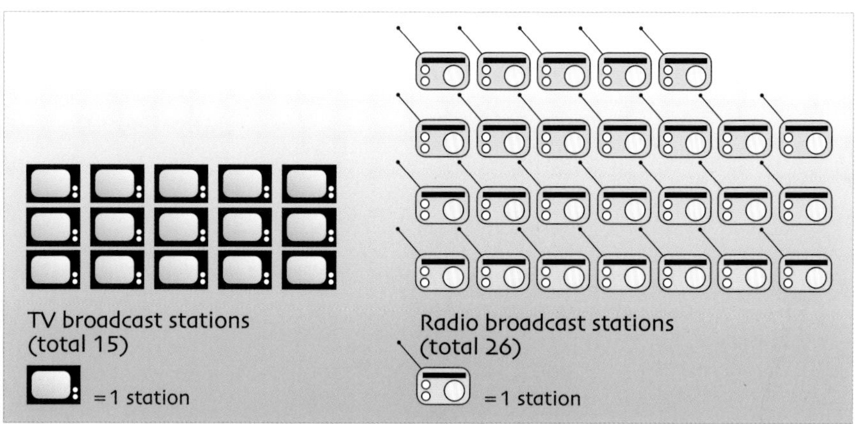

Web Search ▶▶

- **www.comminit.com/strategicthinking/st2002/thinking-386.html**
  Bangladeshi radio.
- **www.discoverybangladesh.com/meetbangladesh/art.html**
  Information about writers, art, music, dance and drama in Bangladesh.

Government

DATABASE

Tax

The government raises taxes to pay for healthcare, housing, transport and so on. Most of the tax comes from customs duties on imported goods. People earning 225,000 takas (£2,410) or more a year pay between 10 and 25 per cent in income tax.

Provinces and Districts

The country is divided into six main administrative areas, called divisions or provinces. These are further divided into districts.

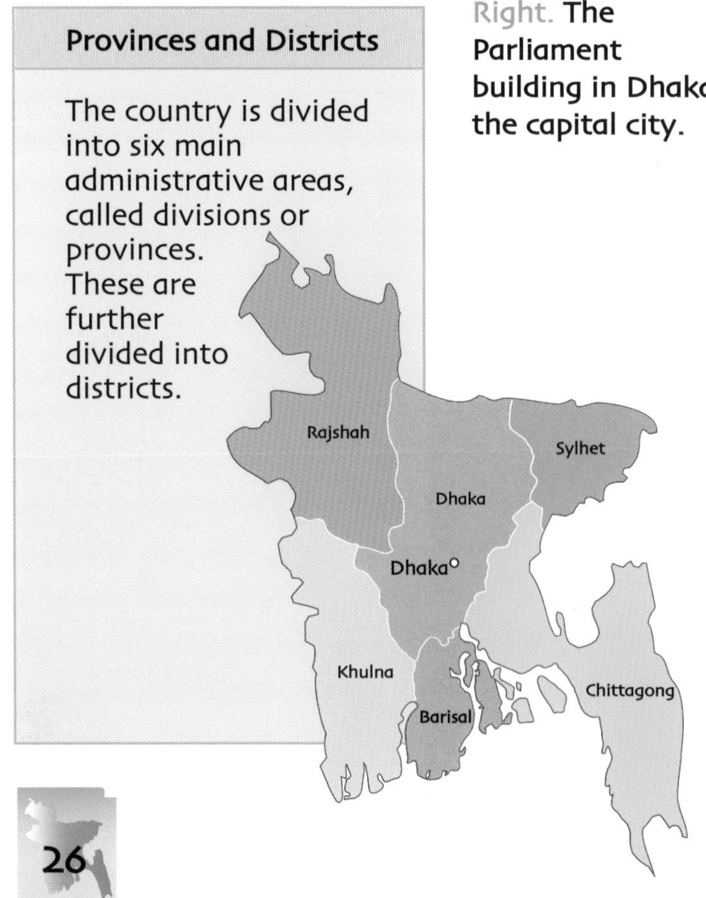

Bangladesh is governed by elected members of Parliament, headed by a prime minister. The president is the official head of state.

President and government

The president and parliament serve for up to five years. There are 300 members of parliament, each of whom is elected by the people of his or her own area. Voting is open to Bangladeshi citizens from the age

Right. **The Parliament building in Dhaka, the capital city.**

of 18. There are several political parties. The party that gains the most seats in the election forms the government. That party's leader, with the president's approval, becomes the prime minister.

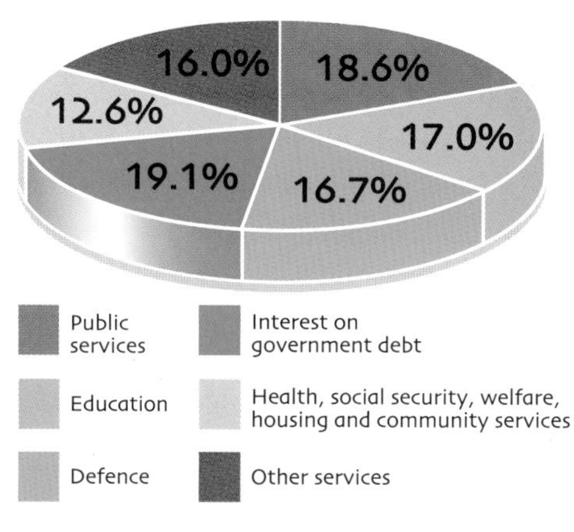

Above. **How the government spends its money and the interest it pays on money borrowed from other countries.**

Religion and free speech

The state religion of Bangladesh is Islam but Muslims are not favoured in any way over followers of other religions. Laws and regulations also state that men and women must be treated equally, that there should be a free press, and that everyone should be allowed freedom of speech.

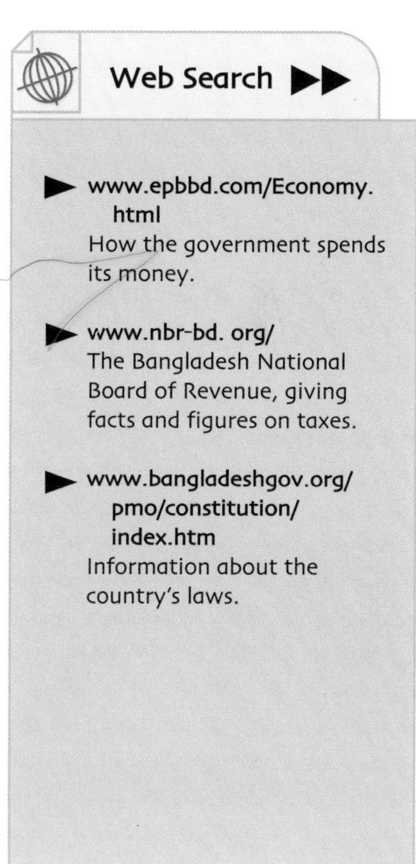

Web Search ▶▶

- **www.epbbd.com/Economy.html**
  How the government spends its money.
- **www.nbr-bd. org/**
  The Bangladesh National Board of Revenue, giving facts and figures on taxes.
- **www.bangladeshgov.org/pmo/constitution/index.htm**
  Information about the country's laws.

Place in the World

DATABASE

Important dates to 1974

500 BCE Tribal people establish kingdom of Vanga (Bengal)

CE 750–1200 Rule by Buddhist and Hindu leaders

1576 Conquered by Muslim Mughul emperor Akbar

1757 British become the new rulers of the Indian subcontinent

1947 British leave and divide subcontinent into India (Hindu) and Pakistan (Muslim). East Bengal becomes part of Pakistan, but with India in between the two parts

1971 Bengali nationalists proclaim independent republic of Bangladesh, and civil war follows. West Pakistan armies defeated with help from India

1972 First government of People's Republic of Bangladesh, with Sheikh Mujibur-Rahman as prime minister

The People's Republic of Bangladesh began in war and revolution in 1971.

Independence and beyond

In 1947, when the British finally left their main colonies in Asia, the region was split in two: India was to be mainly for Hindus, and Pakistan for Muslims. But there were two parts to Pakistan, separated by 1,500 kilometres: West Pakistan and East Pakistan, which was in Bengal.

Below. **The High Court in Dhaka, centre of the legal system.**

In 1971, East Pakistan tried to become independent as Bangladesh. It was attacked by the army of West Pakistan. About three million people were killed before Bangladesh won independence in 1972.

In 1974, it joined the United Nations (UN). Bangladesh also belongs to the British Commonwealth.

Over the last 10 years, Bangladesh's wealth has doubled. By 2010, the country aims to halve the number of its poor people, which stands at about 45 million. To do this, its economy must grow by 48 per cent – this is a big challenge.

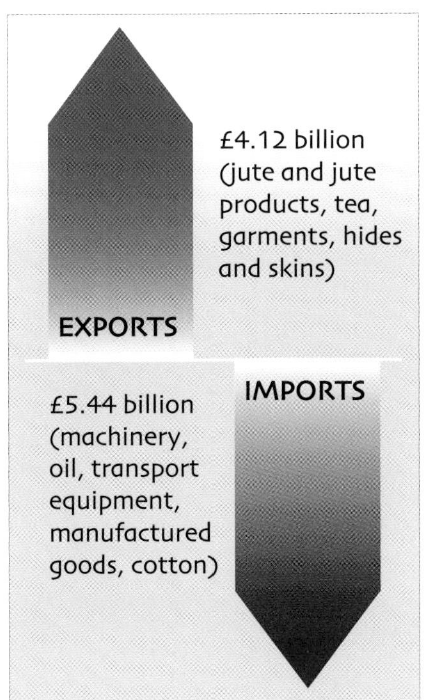

Left. **The value of Bangladesh's exports and imports.**

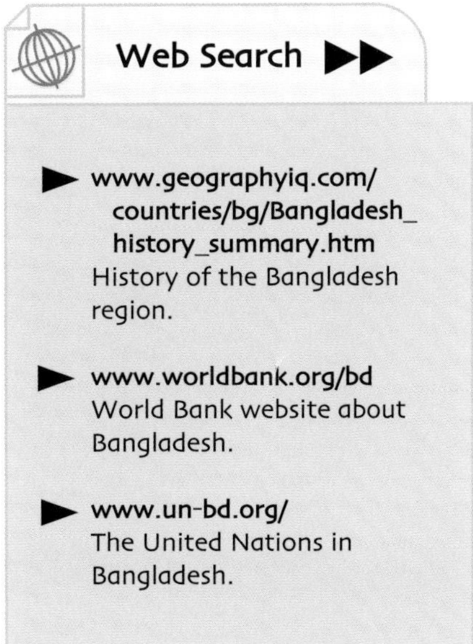

Web Search ▶▶

- **www.geographyiq.com/countries/bg/Bangladesh_history_summary.htm**
  History of the Bangladesh region.
- **www.worldbank.org/bd**
  World Bank website about Bangladesh.
- **www.un-bd.org/**
  The United Nations in Bangladesh.

DATABASE

Important dates since 1974

1974 Bangladesh takes its seat at the UN

1975 Sheikh Mujib assassinated in military takeover. Four years of martial law follow

1981 President Zia Rahman, founder of the Bangladesh National Party (BNP), is assassinated

1986 Parliamentary elections won by Jatiya (People's) Party (JP)

1988 Islam made the state religion. Flooding kills thousands of people and leaves 30 million homeless

1991–96 BNP, led by widow of Zia Rahman, heads government after new elections

1996 BNP re-elected, but Awami League (AL), led by Sheikh Mujib's daughter, forms new government after fresh elections

2001 BNP re-elected after period of strikes

Area:
147,570 sq km

Population size:
133.4 million

Capital city:
Dhaka (population 8,942,300)

Other major cities:
Chittagong (2,592,400), Khulna (1,211,500), Rajshahi (712,400), Gazipur (520,800), Narayaganj (357,300)

Longest river:
Ganges–Padma (part of Ganges) (306 km)

Highest mountain:
Tahjindong (1,412 m)

Currency:
Taka (Tk)

Flag:
The red disc represents the sun of freedom and the blood that was shed to achieve independence. The green background represents the Bangladeshi countryside and is the traditional colour of Islam.

Languages:
Official language: Bangla (Bengali)

Natural resources
Natural gas, coal, lignite, peat, a little oil, limestone, sand, ceramic clay, hard rock, jute, bamboo

Major exports:
Ready-made clothes, jute and jute goods, tea, leather and leather goods, newsprint (paper for newspapers), fish, frozen foods

Some holidays and festivals
1 January: New Year's Day.
Early March (11th lunar month):Pawhela Falgun. 'First Day of Spring' when people attend fairs, exchange greetings, flowers, cards and gifts.
26 March: Independence Day. Anniversary of the declaration of independence from Pakistan in 1971.
Mid-April (1st day, 1st lunar month): Pawhela Boishakh (Bengali New Year). Singing and fairs to mark the beginning of the Bengali New Year.
15 August: Anniversary of the assassination, in 1975, of Sheikh Mujibur-Rahman, the father of the Bangladesh nation.

Official religion:
Islam

Other religions
Hindu 11 per cent,
Buddhist and Christian 0.9 per cent,
Others 0.1 per cent

Key Words

BUDDHISM
Religion based on the teachings of Siddhartha Gautama, also known as the Buddha, who was born in India in 563 BCE.

COMMONWEALTH (OF NATIONS)
Association of independent countries, nearly all of which once belonged to the British Empire.

CROPS
Plants grown for food or for products to sell, such as cotton and jute.

DROUGHT
A long period without rain.

ECONOMY
The business of money, industry and resources.

EXPORTS
Goods or products sold to other countries.

FLOOD
When a river bursts its banks or the sea is blown inland and water covers flat land.

HINDUISM
A 4,000-year-old religion that began in India, and is the major religion of India.

HYDRO-ELECTRIC POWER
Electrical power created from flowing water, such as a river that has been dammed to provide energy for an electricity generator in a power station.

IMPORTS
Goods or products bought in from other countries.

INDEPENDENT
Ruled by people living in the country and not by another country.

ISLAM
Religion begun by Muhammad, the Prophet, in CE 622 in what is today Saudi Arabia.

JUTE
A woody herb and its fibres, grown in river valleys and used to make string, matting, carpets, sacking and other products.

MANGROVES
Leafy tropical trees that grow in shallow, salty water near the coast.

MONSOON
A wind that brings moisture from the sea and deposits it on the land as rain in the summer months.

REPUBLIC
A country whose leaders are elected to govern, rather than, for example, rule by a king or queen, when the power of leadership is handed down through generations.

RESOURCES
A country's supplies of energy, natural materials and minerals.

RICKSHAW
A passenger vehicle powered by bicycle or motor scooter.

SUBCONTINENT
A large land mass, made up of several countries, such as India, Pakistan and Bangladesh, but smaller than the whole continent.

Index